"Breaking Free from the Cycle of Poor Money Choices

THE MINDSET OF BROKE PEOPLE

"Breaking Free from the Cycle of Poor Money Choices

Alan Murphy Jr

"It is not the strongest of the species that survive, nor the most intelligent, but the one most responsive to change." – Charles Darwin

"Breaking Free from the Cycle of Poor Money Choices

Copyright

All rights reserved. No part of this publication may be reproduced, distributed, or transmitted in any form or by any means, including photocopying, recording, or other electronic or mechanical methods, without the prior written permission of the publisher, except in the case of brief quotations embodied in critical reviews and certain other noncommercial uses permitted by copyright law.

Copyright ©ALAN MURPHY JR, 2024

Acknowledgement

I want to start by saying how grateful I am to my dad, Zachary Murphy. This book was built on your lessons, stories, and wise words. Your advice has been very helpful, and your support has been constant. I will always be grateful to you for teaching me how important it is to be smart with money and what happens when you don't.

To my wonderful wife: your unfailing love, support, and patience have been my biggest strength. Thank you for having faith in me and being there for me while I spent hours studying and writing. I really appreciate your love and support.

Thanks to my family and friends for always supporting me and being understanding while I spent a lot of time studying and writing. Your faith in my work kept me going and on track.

I would also like to recognize the people whose stories are presented in this book. Your stories serve as important lessons for all of us. Sharing your journeys—both the successes and the downfalls—provides valuable insights that will help readers make informed financial choices.

"Breaking Free from the Cycle of Poor Money Choices

From The Author

Thank you for picking up "The Mindset of Broke People." This book is designed to help you understand and change financial behaviors that may be holding you back. Reflect on your own financial habits, set clear goals for improvement, practice discipline in your spending, educate yourself continuously, and ensure your financial plans are flexible to adapt to life's changes. Surround yourself with positive influences and focus on long-term benefits rather than instant gratification.

Remember, the path to financial stability and success is a journey, not a destination. Use the lessons and strategies in this book as tools to navigate that journey. Implement them gradually, stay committed, and watch as small changes lead to significant improvements in your financial life. Thank you for allowing me to be a part of your financial journey.

Warm regards,

Alan Murphy Jr.

"Breaking Free from the Cycle of Poor Money Choices

Table Of Contents

Introduction: Good Old Tom........................8
Chapter 1: The Ignorance Trap....................11
    The Role of Financial Education in Wealth Preservation..13
    Building a Strong Financial Foundation............13
    The Broader Implications of Financial Education..15

Chapter 2: Instant Gratification Dilemma....22
What is Instant Gratification?....................22
    The psychological effect of quick satisfaction..23
    The Impact of Instant Gratification on Financial Decisions..24
    Strategies for Managing Instant Gratification. 27

Chapter 3: The Debt Spiral........................30
The Role of Loans.. 30
    The Consequences of Debt Accumulation........34
    Strategies for Managing and Preventing Debt Accumulation... 37

Chapter 4: The Lifestyle Inflation Pitfall... 39
    The Consequences of Overspending..................42
    The Role of Financial Discipline........................43

Chapter 5: The Investment Mirage............ 46
    The Importance of Financial Planning..............46
    Common Pitfalls in Financial Planning........... 48

Chapter 6: The Planning Paradox..............55

Understanding Investment Choices.................. 55
The Consequences of Poor Investment Choices... 57
Chapter 7: The Environmental Influence.. 64
The Power of Environmental Influences.......... 64
Chapter 8: The Adaptability Factor 71
The Universal Importance of Adaptability....... 71
Adaptability in Financial Matters..................... 72
Chapter 9: The Psychological Battlefield.... 78
The Psychological Impact of Money................. 78
The Role of Emotions in Financial Decisions... 79
Recap And Reflection.............................. 85

"Breaking Free from the Cycle of Poor Money Choices

Introduction: Good Old Tom

I remember my dad's friend very well. We'll call him Tom. Tom used to be one of the wealthiest people in our town. Many people wished they had his life. He really lived up to the phrase "live fast." Tom's life was full of luxury and spending, and he never missed a chance to brag about the latest expensive treat he had bought for himself.

When Tom walked into a bar, everyone looked at him. He would pay for everyone's drinks, and he wouldn't think twice about the huge bills. My dad used to tell me stories about how Tom spent a lot of money. One that always stood out was the time Tom spent almost $900,000 on cars for a bunch of hot women he had no plans to marry. It was all for show, to keep up the appearance of being rich and successful.

But beneath the surface, Tom's financial base was collapsing. His dogged chase of wealth, the constant need to please others, and the lack of any real financial planning led to his eventual failure. It wasn't long before the money ran out. Tom went bankrupt, losing everything he had worked for. My father, out of love and kindness, has been helping him little by little to get back on his feet.

Tom's story is a stark reminder of how fleeting wealth can be when it's not handled wisely. It also serves as a strong lesson about the risks of financial mishandling and the bad choices that can lead even the best among us to ruin. This book, "The Mindset of Broke People," is my attempt to turn Tom's story—and many others like it—into a useful tool for others.

The stories and ideas in this book hope to highlight the common mistakes that lead to financial downfall. Through the lens of real-life case studies, we'll take a deep dive into the lives of those who started off rich but ended up broke. We'll examine the decisions they made, the dangers they fell into, and the psychological traps that trapped them.

This book isn't just about pointing out what went wrong; it's about learning from these mistakes. By knowing the habits and choices that lead to financial ruin, we can set a different path for ourselves. We can make better choices, avoid the usual mistakes, and build a more safe financial future.

"Breaking Free from the Cycle of Poor Money Choices

So, as you turn these pages, think of it as a TV screen showing you the lives of those who have walked the path of financial ruin. Watch closely, learn from their experiences, and use these lessons to steer clear of the same fate. Let's dig into the thoughts that lead to being broke and discover how to develop habits that lead to long financial well-being.

"Breaking Free from the Cycle of Poor Money Choices

Chapter 1: The Ignorance Trap

Let me take you back to a story that deeply shaped my understanding of financial education. It's about Sean Quinn, once Ireland's richest man. Quinn's tale is a strong example of how a lack of financial knowledge can turn the biggest financial stars into mere shadows of their former selves. His story is not just a telling of personal failure but a crucial lesson on why financial education is so vital.

The Case Of Sean Quinn

I remember reading about Sean Quinn's rise with awe. Born in County Cavan, Ireland, Quinn started from poor roots. He began his work in the early 1970s with a small sand business. His drive and hard work pushed him into the spotlight, and he soon became an important person in Ireland's business world. His businesses were varied, ranging from real estate to insurance, and he seemed unbeatable.

To many, Quinn was the image of financial success. He lived a life of luxury, his wealth seemingly endless. His businesses were thriving, and he was a figure of victory. But looking back, it's clear that beneath this mask of success was a critical oversight—an ignorance of fundamental financial education.

The story took a dramatic turn when Quinn invested heavily in Anglo Irish Bank. In the early 2000s, Quinn started buying sizable shares in the bank, a move that originally looked to be a stroke of genius. The bank's performance was strong at first, which must have boosted Quinn's faith. However, his knowledge of the business was shallow.

I've always thought about how easy it is to get swept up in the joy of financial success. Quinn's position is a great case of this. His purchases were driven by a mix of overconfidence and a lack of deep financial knowledge. As the global financial disaster of 2008 developed, Anglo Irish Bank was hit hard, and so was Quinn. His possessions, once thought valuable, fell in value.

The failure of the bank wasn't just a financial loss; it was a stark reveal of Quinn's lack of financial understanding. His failure to grasp the complexities of the financial markets and handle risks effectively led to his downfall. The once-wealthy businessman faced bankruptcy, his company falling under the weight of poor financial choices.

The Role of Financial Education in Wealth Preservation

This story is a clear example of why financial education is so crucial. Financial literacy isn't just a set of vague ideas; it's about knowing how to handle, spend, and protect money. It includes learning how to budget, save, and make educated financial decisions.

Think about it: If Sean Quinn had a good background in financial education, he might have handled his purchases differently. He would have known the risks involved and made steps to reduce them. Financial education gives the skills to manage the complicated world of finance and make choices that fit with long-term goals.

For many, financial education starts with basic principles—creating a budget, knowing credit, and learning about investment options. But it goes deeper. It includes knowing the details of financial markets, recognizing the effect of economic events, and changing tactics as circumstances change.

Building a Strong Financial Foundation

From my own viewpoint, building a strong financial base starts with gaining a thorough understanding of financial concepts. This schooling doesn't come from a single source but through a mix of learning ways. Reading books on personal finance, taking online classes, and speaking with financial advisers are all ways to build knowledge.

Creating and sticking to a budget plan is important. This plan should cover everything from budgets to long-term investing techniques. It should be flexible to changes in the financial situation and include methods for controlling risks. Practical experience, such as tracking costs and making financial goals, strengthens this information and helps develop a better understanding of financial concepts.

Reflecting on Quinn's experience, I see several key lessons. Firstly, constant learning is important. Financial schooling isn't a one-time event but a lifelong process. Staying updated about financial issues and adapting to changes in the financial world can prevent costly mistakes.

Secondly, overconfidence can be a dangerous trait in financial decision-making. Even wealthy people like Quinn can fall victim to their own pride if they're not grounded in financial reality. Humility and a desire to learn are important for sound financial management.

Lastly, knowing the nature of investments and their related risks is vital. Investments should be treated with careful study and a clear understanding of possible results. High-risk projects require careful thought and control to escape major losses.

The Broader Implications of Financial Education

The importance of financial education goes beyond individual success. On a wider scale, financial knowledge adds to economic security and growth. Individuals who understand financial concepts are better prepared to make choices that benefit their personal well-being and the business as a whole.

Moreover, better financial knowledge can help solve financial inequality. By offering access to financial knowledge and tools, people from different backgrounds can improve their financial situations and work toward greater economic equality.

As I think about Sean Quinn's story and the larger effects of financial education, it becomes clear that gaining financial knowledge is not just helpful but necessary for anyone looking to keep and grow their wealth. Let's explore some useful ways to gain financial education and apply what you learn in your financial journey.

1. Formal Education: Building a Solid Foundation

One effective way to gain financial knowledge is through traditional education. Many universities and schools give classes in personal finance, economics, and business techniques. Enrolling in these classes can provide an organized learning experience and a complete understanding of financial ideas.

Formal schooling helps build a strong basis in financial concepts. Courses often cover important subjects such as planning, saving, investment, and controlling debt. For those starting their financial journey, formal schooling offers a clear road to understanding complicated financial systems and making educated choices.

2. Self-Study: Books and Online Resources

Self-study is another useful way for getting financial information. There is an extensive collection of books and online tools available that cover different financial issues. Books by famous experts in personal finance and business offer deep insights into handling money effectively.

Online sites such as Coursera, Udemy, and Khan Academy provide a wealth of classes on financial issues. These tools allow people to learn at their own pace and dig into topics of personal interest. Investing time in reading financial books and taking online classes can greatly improve one's understanding of financial management.

3. **Financial Seminars and Workshops:** Attending financial classes and training can offer useful information and insights into current financial trends. These events often feature expert speakers who share their experiences and methods for financial success.

Seminars and classes provide an engaging learning experience, allowing guests to ask questions and participate in conversations. They also offer networking chances, connecting people with others interested in financial subjects. Participating in these events can improve knowledge and provide new views on financial management.

4. **Consulting with Financial Advisors:** Consulting with financial experts can offer personalized advice geared to individual financial situations. Financial planners help build complete financial plans, offer investment advice, and provide insights into controlling risks.

Working with a financial planner can provide useful help in managing the difficulties of financial markets. Advisors bring knowledge and experience to the table, helping people make informed choices and build plans matched with their financial goals.

5. Practical Experience: Applying Financial Knowledge Acquiring financial education is only part of the issue; applying what is learned is important for achieving financial success. Starting with simple practices like making a budget can help track income and spending, giving a better picture of one's financial position.

Implementing methods for saving and spending is another important aspect. Setting financial goals, such as building an emergency fund or saving for retirement, and making a plan to achieve them can help handle expenses successfully. Diversifying investments and measuring risks are key elements of applying financial knowledge.

6. Continuous Learning: Staying Updated: Financial schooling is a constant process. The financial world is constantly changing, with new trends and changes emerging regularly. Staying updated about these changes is crucial for making good financial choices.

Subscribing to financial news sites, following reliable financial blogs, and joining in online groups can help keep up with the latest information. Continuous learning ensures that people stay aware of market trends and can change their financial plans accordingly.

7. Learning from Mistakes: Embracing Financial Lessons Learning from financial mistakes is a strong way to gain insights and improve decision-making. Reflecting on past financial choices, both successful and failed, offers important lessons.

Analyzing what went wrong in earlier financial projects and understanding the factors that led to those results can help improve strategies and avoid making the same mistakes. Embracing these lessons is important for personal growth and financial gain.

8. Networking with Peers: Sharing Knowledge Networking with people who share an interest in finance can provide additional ideas and support. Engaging with others in financial conversations allows for the sharing of ideas, experiences, and tactics.

Joining financial clubs, online communities, or local investing groups can enable these relationships. Networking helps broaden views and gives chances to learn from others who have different financial experiences.

9. Leveraging Technology: Financial Tools and Apps Technology offers a range of tools and apps meant to improve financial management. Budgeting apps, investment tools, and financial planning software can help in keeping prepared and making informed choices.

Using these tools can simplify financial management processes, giving real-time views into spending, saves, and investing. Leveraging technology helps keep control over financial actions and supports better decision-making.

Chapter 2: The Instant Gratification Dilemma

Instant satisfaction is a strong force that can influence our financial choices and general economic well-being. It is the desire for instant gains and the tendency to favor short-term joys over long-term benefits. This desire often pushes people to make financial choices that may seem rewarding in the moment but can lead to major effects down the line. Understanding this idea is crucial for keeping financial security and making good choices.

What is Instant Gratification?

Instant pleasure refers to the urge to seek instant satisfaction rather than waiting for a more rewarding result. In financial terms, it appears as a desire for spending now rather than saving for the future, or following quick gains rather than investing in long-term growth. This behavior can be seen in various parts of financial life, from consumer buying to investment techniques.

The appeal of quick satisfaction often stems from a psychological need for rapid benefits and the pleasure gained from instant success. The quick pleasure or prize gives a sense of success or happiness, albeit briefly. However, this instant happiness can come at the cost of long-term financial health and security.

The psychological effect of quick satisfaction

- **Dopamine Response:** Instant satisfaction causes the release of dopamine, a neurotransmitter linked with happiness and reward. This chemical reaction supports the behavior, making it more appealing to seek instant benefits.

- **Short-Term Focus:** Individuals driven by quick satisfaction often focus on short-term benefits rather than long-term effects. This short-term focus can cloud judgment and lead to choices that value instant pleasure over future security.

- **Emotional Spending:** The need for quick pleasure can lead to emotional spending, where individuals make purchases or financial choices based on mood or emotional states rather than sensible analysis.

The Impact of Instant Gratification on Financial Decisions

- **Increased Debt:** Individuals who value quick benefits may depend on credit cards or loans to support their wants. This dependence on debt can build over time, leading to financial pressure and trouble handling returns.

- **Poor Investment Choices:** Seeking quick profits can lead to reckless investment choices, such as risky trading or investing in high-risk projects. These decisions often lack thorough research and can result in significant financial losses.

- **Neglect of Savings and Planning:** The focus on instant satisfaction can overshadow the value of saving and financial planning. Individuals may ignore payments to retirement accounts or emergency funds, risking long-term financial security.

Case Study Of Vera Wang

To show the effect of quick satisfaction, let's examine the case of Vera Wang, a prominent fashion designer known for her famous wedding gowns and luxurious designs. Despite her success, Wang's early business growth faced hurdles based on the desire for fast success.

Vera Wang's rise in the fashion business was rapid. Her brand quickly gained fame, and the excitement of this success led her to follow bold growth plans. Wang's drive to capitalize on instant success led to a series of rapid business decisions aimed at growing her operations.

The original success of Wang's brand developed a strong desire for quick results. The draw of fast growth was tempting, and Wang followed it with zeal. However, this drive for quick success led to several financial difficulties:

Overextension of Resources: Wang's desire for instant growth led to overextending financial resources. Expanding the business quickly needed sizable investments in new sites, people, and operating infrastructure.

Operational Challenges: The fast growth put a strain on the business's operational processes. Managing greater demand, building up output, and keeping quality control became major obstacles.

Financial Strain: The financial effects of rapid growth included higher overhead costs and the need for substantial cash. Without proper financial planning, the business faced problems in handling cash flow and continuing activities.

Vera Wang's experience gives important lessons in managing the desire for quick gratification:

- **Strategic Growth:** Sustainable growth needs careful planning and thought. Instead of jumping into fast development, build a smart growth plan that fits with long-term goals and ensures that resources are allocated effectively.

- **Financial Planning:** Implement a complete financial plan that includes planning, estimating, and risk management.

Proper financial planning helps minimize the risks connected with quick development and ensures that growth is doable.

- **Operational Efficiency:** Focus on better operational efficiency to meet greater demand. Streamline processes, invest in technology, and ensure that systems are in place to support growth without losing quality.

- **Long-Term Vision:** Embrace a long-term vision that values steady, lasting progress over instant benefits. Cultivating patience and keeping a focus on long-term goals helps escape the dangers of quick satisfaction.

Strategies for Managing Instant Gratification

To combat the desire for quick satisfaction and make more informed financial choices, try the following strategies:

- **Set Clear Financial Goals:** Establish clear, long-term financial goals that provide direction and drive. Break down these goals into smaller, doable steps to keep focus and track progress.

- **Create a Budget:** Develop a budget that fits with your financial goals and values saving and spending. A well-structured budget helps control spending and ensures that resources are allocated effectively.

- **Practice Delayed Gratification:** Cultivate the habit of delaying instant gains in favor of long-term benefits. For example, save for a wanted buy rather than depending on credit, or invest in assets that build wealth over time.

- **Teach Yourself:** Continuously teach yourself about financial concepts and tactics. Knowledge allows you to make educated choices and avoid the desire of hasty spending.

- **Seek Professional Advice:** Consult with financial advisors to gain insights and advice on handling growth and making sound financial choices. Professional advice can provide useful support and help manage complicated financial conditions.

Chapter 3: The Debt Spiral

Before diving into the dangers of collecting debt, it's important to explain the link between loans and debt. Loans are a form of debt, usually taken out to pay projects, purchases, or personal costs. They involve taking a specific amount of money with the understanding to return it, often with interest, over a set time.

The Role of Loans

Loans can serve as a valuable financial tool when used carefully. They can help people and companies handle cash flow, invest in chances, or make major purchases that might be out of reach otherwise. The key to using loans successfully is ensuring that they are doable and match with long-term financial goals.

However, when loans are mishandled or piled overly, they can add to financial trouble. The difference between responsible borrowing and damaging debt buildup lies in how loans are used and handled. Responsible borrowing includes a clear plan for payback and a full understanding of the financial effects.

Successful Individuals Who Started with Loans

To show how loans can be used as a tool for success, consider the stories of these two rich people who began their journeys with borrowed capital:

1. Richard Branson

Richard Branson, the founder of the Virgin Group, is a famous example of someone who leveraged loans successfully. Branson started his business journey with a student magazine, which was supported by a small loan. As he expanded his ventures into the music industry with Virgin Records, he continued to use loans to pay his business growth.

Branson's success with Virgin Records and later efforts in fields such as planes and space travel shows how smart use of loans can drive major business success. His ability to handle debt properly and invest in growth opportunities led to the creation of a global brand.

2. Elon Musk

Elon Musk, the founder of companies like Tesla and SpaceX, also began his trip with stolen funds. Musk spent his personal savings and took out loans to fund the early stages of Tesla Motors and SpaceX. His desire to leverage debt for high-risk, high-reward projects played a crucial role in turning these companies into industry stars.

Musk's success shows how taking measured chances with loans, when combined with new vision and effective management, can lead to substantial achievements. His ability to balance debt with business growth and strategic planning has been important in his financial success.

The Case Study Of Björgólfur Guðmundsson

While loans can indeed be a spark for success, their abuse or excessive buildup can lead to financial ruin. The story of Björgólfur Guðmundsson, an Icelandic businessman, illustrates the dark side of debt buildup. His experience serves as a warning tale of how debt, when ignored, can result in serious financial effects.

Björgólfur Guðmundsson's rise in the business world was marked by bold growth and active borrowing. Known for his ownership of Landsbanki, an Icelandic bank, Guðmundsson's story is a sharp warning of how accumulating debt without proper financial controls can lead to catastrophic results.

In the early days of his work, Guðmundsson's success led him to explore fast growth possibilities. The joy of growth and the hope of future gains drove him to borrow significant sums to fund different projects. This bold approach to growth showed a strong desire to capitalize on instant success and capitalize on market possibilities.

However, the dependence on borrowed funds caused a risky financial position. Debt, when accumulated without proper planning and risk management, can become overwhelming. For Guðmundsson, this meant taking on more debt to support extra growth, which eventually led to the collapse of his business company.

The failure of Landsbanki is a notable example of how excessive debt can lead to financial ruin. Guðmundsson's bold growth tactics and dependence on borrowed funds put the bank in a weak situation. The global financial crisis of 2008 worsened these risks, showing the weaknesses in the bank's financial structure.

Landsbanki's downfall was not solely due to external economic conditions but also showed internal financial mishandling and over-leverage. The failure to handle debt successfully and adapt to changing market conditions led to the bank's collapse, resulting in major losses for investors and stakeholders.

The Consequences of Debt Accumulation

- **Financial Instability:** High amounts of debt cause financial instability, making it difficult to handle cash flow and meet payback commitments. This uncertainty can lead to missed payments, higher interest costs, and ultimate bankruptcy.

- **Credit Risk:** Excessive debt affects credit scores and buying ability. A high debt-to-income ratio results in higher interest rates and lower access to loans, complicated financial management.

- **Increased Stress:** The load of handling large debt often leads to stress and worry, hurting mental and physical well-being. The pressure of debt can impact decision-making and general quality of life.

Björgólfur Guðmundsson's story offers important lessons on handling debt and avoiding financial pitfalls:

- **Understand the Risks of Debt:** Recognize the risks involved with debt buildup. Before borrowing, consider the possible effect on financial health and ensure that debt amounts are reasonable.

- **Maintain a Balanced Debt-to-Income Ratio:** Avoid over-leveraging by having debt levels equal to income. This balance helps keep financial security and lowers the risk of failure.

- **Develop a Repayment Plan:** Create a clear payback plan describing how borrowed funds will be repaid. Regularly review and change the plan to stay on track and handle debt effectively.

- **Avoid Impulsive Borrowing:** Resist the urge to borrow recklessly. Evaluate whether the debt is important and fits with long-term financial goals before taking on new loans.

- **Monitor Financial Health:** Regularly track financial state, including debt amounts and cash flow. Staying informed helps control debt successfully and address problems quickly.

- **Seek Professional Advice:** Consult with financial advisors to gain insights on controlling debt and creating strategies. Professional advice can help handle complicated financial problems and improve security.

- **Build an Emergency Fund:** Establish and keep an emergency fund to cover unexpected costs. An emergency fund lowers the need for loans in times of disaster and offers financial protection.

Strategies for Managing and Preventing Debt Accumulation

- **Create a Budget**: Develop a complete budget that describes income, spending, and savings goals. A budget helps control spending, track debt payments, and divide resources effectively.

- **Prioritize Debt Repayment:** Focus on returning high-interest debt first to lower total debt costs. Prioritize debt reduction as a key financial goal and apply extra funds towards lowering remaining amounts.

- **Use Debt Wisely:** Use debt wisely for investments or important costs rather than for non-essential purchases. Ensure that any debt acquired fits with financial goals.

- **Maintain Financial Discipline:** Practice strict financial habits to avoid needless debt. Mindful spending, regular saves, and

"Breaking Free from the Cycle of Poor Money Choices

avoiding credit for daily costs add to financial health.

Chapter 4: The Lifestyle Inflation Pitfall

Overspending is often the result of a variety of habits and behavioral traits that lead people to spend more than they can afford. Understanding these habits is crucial for spotting and solving wasting patterns before they become harmful to financial security. Here are some common habits that lead to overspending:

- **Impulse Purchases:** The habit of making random purchases without considering their impact on the budget can lead to significant overspending. These hasty choices are often driven by feelings, rewards, or the desire for quick satisfaction.

- **Living Beyond Means:** This habit involves constantly spending more money than is made. Individuals who live beyond their means frequently depend on credit cards or loans to pay for their lifestyle, leading to a circle of debt and financial pressure.

- **Keeping Up with the Joneses:** The desire to match or beat the lifestyle of peers, friends, or celebrities can drive unnecessary spending. This habit often results in buying high-end things or services to project a certain image, rather than based on personal wants or financial capability.

- **Lack of Budgeting:** Failing to build and stick to a budget can result in uncontrolled spending. Without a clear financial plan, people may not track costs effectively and may spend beyond their means.

- **Overindulgence in Luxuries:** Prioritizing expensive things or events over important costs and funds can lead to financial problems. Overspending on non-essential things can weaken financial security and prevent long-term financial goals from being met.

Several high-profile people have faced financial problems or near bankruptcy due to excessive spending. These cases show the serious effects of living beyond one's means:

Mike Tyson

Former heavyweight boxing winner Mike Tyson is a well-known example of someone who faced financial ruin due to overspending. Despite making hundreds of millions of dollars throughout his career, Tyson's expensive lifestyle—including homes, fancy cars, and extravagant parties—led to substantial financial losses. His failure to handle his finances properly ended in bankruptcy in 2003.

Lindsay Lohan

Actress Lindsay Lohan also faced financial problems due to overspending. Known for her high-profile lifestyle and frequent legal problems, Lohan's excessive spending on personal pleasures and legal fees added to her financial insecurity. Despite her job gains, her financial mishandling and lifestyle choices led to significant debt and court problems.

The Case Study Of Patricia Kluge

Understanding the effect of overspending and living inflation becomes easier through the story of Patricia Kluge. Kluge's experience offers a clear example of how living beyond one's means can lead to serious financial effects Patricia Kluge's story is a powerful example of how overspending and lifestyle inflation can spin out of control. As a famous lady and former wife of Donald Trump, Kluge was accustomed to a life of wealth and opulence. Her expensive lifestyle, paired with bad financial management, eventually led to personal bankruptcy and the sale of her winery.

In the 1990s, Patricia Kluge accepted a lifestyle that included expensive home improvements, luxury cars, and high-end personal costs. The buying of a big farm and the creation of Kluge farm Winery were major financial responsibilities that showed her desire for an extravagant lifestyle.

However, Kluge's financial problems began when her spending habits outpaced her income and business revenue. The costs involved with keeping a big farm, having a winery, and delighting in luxury items became unaffordable. Her failure to handle costs effectively led to financial strain.

The Consequences of Overspending

Financial Strain: The gap between Kluge's income and spending increased, causing major financial pressure. The high costs of keeping her farm and winery put a strain on her resources.

sale and Bankruptcy: The financial strain eventually led to the sale of Kluge's farm and personal bankruptcy. Despite her high-profile rank and substantial wealth, her failure to control spending effectively led to the loss of major assets.

The Role of Financial Discipline

Addressing overspending and lifestyle inflation requires financial discipline and a dedication to controlling costs sensibly. Here are methods to help create and keep financial discipline:

- **Create a Realistic Budget:** Developing a thorough budget is crucial for controlling expenses and avoiding lifestyle inflation. A budget should describe income, necessary costs, and savings goals, helping people stay on track and avoid splurging.

- **Set Clear Financial Goals:** Establish clear financial goals, such as saving for retirement, buying a home, or building a backup fund. Prioritize these goals over instant living changes to keep focus and discipline.

- **Monitor Spending Habits:** Regularly review buying habits to spot areas of overspending and make necessary changes. Tracking costs helps keep control over funds and stops living inflation.

- **Practice Mindful Spending:** Be intentional about spending choices and avoid rash purchases. Consider whether each cost fits with financial goals and general budget before making a buy.

- **Avoid Lifestyle Comparisons:** Resist the desire to keep up with others or present a certain image. Focus on personal financial goals and needs rather than external forces or social standards.

- **Build Financial Resilience:** Develop financial resilience by keeping an emergency fund and avoiding dependence on credit for everyday costs. Financial stability helps handle unexpected costs and lowers the need for loans.

- **Seek Professional Guidance:** Consult with financial experts for personalized help and tactics. Professional advice can help build effective financial plans and improve general financial health.

Chapter 5: The Investment Mirage

Financial planning is a crucial aspect of controlling one's income and achieving a secure future. It includes setting financial goals, building strategies to achieve those goals, and regularly reviewing and changing plans to ensure they stay effective.

Neglecting financial planning can lead to significant financial uncertainty, as it leaves people unprepared for unforeseen costs, market changes, and other financial challenges. This chapter looks deep into the importance of financial planning, shows common mistakes, and studies the case of Eike Batista, whose lack of financial insight led to a dramatic fall from glory.

The Importance of Financial Planning

Effective financial planning provides a path for achieving financial security and long-term goals. It encompasses various components, including budgeting, saving, investing, tax planning, and retirement planning. Here are some key reasons why financial planning is essential:

- **Goal Setting and Achievement:** Financial planning helps individuals set realistic financial goals and build methods to achieve them. Whether it's buying a home, funding education, or retiring comfortably, a well-structured plan offers direction and motivation.

- **Risk Management:** Financial planning includes assessing potential risks and creating strategies to mitigate them. This includes building emergency funds, obtaining insurance, and diversifying investments to protect against market volatility.

- **Debt Management:** Effective financial planning incorporates methods for managing and reducing debt. By prioritizing debt repayment and avoiding unnecessary spending, individuals can achieve greater financial security.

- **Tax Efficiency:** Proper financial planning helps minimize tax liabilities through smart investments and tax-efficient savings plans.

This allows individuals to retain more of their earnings and grow their wealth.

- **Retirement Preparedness:** Financial planning ensures that individuals are adequately prepared for retirement. By setting aside sufficient funds and choosing appropriate investment vehicles, individuals can secure a comfortable retirement.

Common Pitfalls in Financial Planning

Despite its importance, many people neglect financial planning due to various reasons. Here are some common mistakes that can lead to financial instability:

- **Procrastination:** Delaying financial planning can result in missed opportunities and poor preparation for future expenses. The earlier individuals start planning, the better prepared they are to achieve their goals.

- **Lack of Clear Goals:** Without clear financial goals, it becomes difficult to build effective strategies. Vague or undefined goals can lead to inconsistent and unfocused financial planning.

- **Failure to Monitor and Adjust:** Financial plans require regular review and adjustment to remain relevant. Ignoring changes in income, expenses, or market conditions can render a financial plan ineffective.

- **Overleveraging:** Taking on excessive debt without a clear repayment plan can lead to financial strain. Overleveraging can magnify losses and increase the risk of bankruptcy during economic downturns.

- **Ignoring Professional Advice:** Failing to seek advice from financial professionals can result in poor decisions. Professional guidance can provide valuable insights and help navigate complex financial situations.

The Case Study Of Eike Batista

Eike Batista's story is a powerful example of the consequences of neglecting financial planning. Once one of the richest men in Brazil, Batista's empire fell due to poor financial management and overleveraging. His failure provides important lessons on the importance of financial planning and discipline.

Eike Batista was a Brazilian entrepreneur and businessman who amassed vast wealth through his investments in natural resources, including oil and mining. At his peak, Batista was worth an estimated $30 billion, making him one of the richest people in the world. His ambitions were grand, and he envisioned building one of the world's largest corporations.

Despite his vast wealth and success, Batista's empire was built on shaky foundations. His aggressive expansion plans were heavily reliant on debt, and he failed to adopt prudent financial planning to manage this leverage. Several key factors led to his downfall:

- **Overleveraging:** Batista's companies took on massive amounts of debt to fund their operations and expansion. This overleveraging left his businesses vulnerable to market fluctuations and operational failures.

- **Poor Risk Management:** Batista's projects, particularly in the oil industry, encountered significant operational challenges and delays. These issues, coupled with falling commodity prices, exacerbated financial pressure.

- **Lack of Diversification:** A significant portion of Batista's wealth was tied to his energy and mining ventures. The lack of diversification exposed him to sector-specific risks, which materialized as global commodity prices declined.

- **Inadequate Contingency Planning:** Batista did not have adequate contingency plans to address potential setbacks. The absence of a robust financial safety net amplified the impact of business and market challenges.

Batista's financial troubles began to surface in 2012, as his flagship company, OGX, faced production delays and failed to meet its output targets. The company's stock plummeted, and Batista's net worth rapidly declined. By 2013, OGX had filed for bankruptcy, marking one of the largest corporate failures in Latin American history. Batista's other businesses also suffered, leading to a cascade effect that decimated his wealth.

Eike Batista's experience underscores the critical importance of financial planning and prudent risk management. Here are some key lessons from his downfall:

- **Avoid Overleveraging:** While debt can be a useful tool for growth, it should be managed carefully. Overleveraging increases exposure to market volatility and operational challenges. Maintain a balance between debt and equity to minimize risk.

- **Implement Risk Management Strategies:** Develop comprehensive risk management strategies to address potential setbacks. This includes contingency planning, insurance, and diversification to protect against sector-specific risks.

- **Regularly Review Financial Plans:** Financial plans should be dynamic and regularly reviewed to stay current. Monitor changes in income, expenses, and market conditions to make necessary adjustments.

- **Seek Professional Advice:** Consult with financial professionals to gain insights and guidance. Professional advice can help build effective strategies and navigate complex financial situations.

- **Diversify Investments:** Avoid concentrating wealth in a single asset or industry. Diversification helps spread risk and protect against significant losses from any single investment.

Practical Steps for Effective Financial Planning

To avoid the pitfalls of neglecting financial planning, consider the following practical steps:

- **Build an Emergency Fund:** Establish an emergency fund to cover unexpected expenses. Aim for three to six months' worth of living expenses to provide a financial safety net.
- **Invest Wisely:** Develop an investment strategy that aligns with your risk tolerance and financial goals. Diversify investments to spread risk and seek professional advice for informed decision-making.

- **Plan for Retirement:** Start planning for retirement early. Utilize retirement accounts, such as 401(k)s and IRAs, to build a nest egg and take advantage of tax benefits.

- **Review and Adjust Plans Regularly:** Regularly review financial plans and make adjustments as needed. Stay informed about changes in income, expenses, and market conditions to ensure plans remain relevant.

Chapter 6: The Planning Paradox

Investing is a key component of financial growth and security. When done wisely, it can greatly increase one's wealth and provide financial protection. However, making bad business choices can lead to terrible losses and financial ruin.

This chapter discusses the effect of bad investment choices, the importance of due research, and the infamous case of Bernard Madoff, whose Ponzi scheme brought financial devastation to countless investors.

Understanding Investment Choices

Investing involves putting money into various financial tools, such as stocks, bonds, real estate, or businesses, with the hope of creating a return. While all investments carry some amount of risk, choosing informed and smart investment choices can minimize these risks and maximize possible rewards. Poor financial decisions often come from a lack of understanding, poor study, or the draw of high yields without considering the related risks.

Growing up, my father was always careful about his business choices. He wasn't just careful; he was knowledgeable. He spent hours reading financial reports, studying market trends, and getting help from seasoned investors. His dedication paid off in many ways. I remember how he used to talk about the early days when he invested in a small technology business. It wasn't a choice he made lightly. He pored over their business plan, inspected their financial records, and even met with the company's management team. It was a well-informed choice that produced large gains, securing our family's financial future.

My father's success wasn't just a stroke of luck; it was the result of thorough study and careful decision-making. He always stressed the importance of knowing what you're investing in. "Never put your money into something you don't understand," he would say. This concept became a cornerstone of his business plan and one he was keen to pass on to me.

From a young age, my father involved me in his business operations. He would show me how to read financial records, explain market trends, and talk about the possible risks and benefits of different assets. These lessons were priceless and ingrained in me a deep respect for the importance of financial education and due research. Thanks to his advice, I learned to approach buying with a critical and informed attitude, escaping the traps that have trapped many others.

The Consequences of Poor Investment Choices

- **Financial Losses:** The most obvious effect of bad business choices is the loss of money. Depending on the size of the investment, these losses can be large and tough to recover from.

- **Emotional Stress:** Financial losses from bad choices can lead to major emotional stress and worry. The fear of losing more money can result in rushed and illogical choices, further worsening the problem.

- **Reduced Future possibilities:** Financial losses can limit one's ability to spend in future possibilities. The cash that could have been used for other assets or financial goals is reduced, slowing total financial growth.
- **Erosion of Trust**: Poor investment choices can weaken trust in financial institutions,

managers, or markets. This loss of trust can make individuals more hesitant to spend in the future, possibly missing out on profitable chances.

- **Impact on ties**: Financial worry and losses can harm ties with family, friends, and business partners. Disagreements over money and business choices can lead to fights and ruined relationship

Several common mistakes can lead to bad investing choices:

- **Lack of due diligence:** Failing to fully study and understand an investment can result in poor choices. Due diligence includes studying the investment's possible dangers, returns, and total success.

- **Chasing High yields:** The draw of high yields can lead buyers to ignore the related risks. Investments offering extremely high yields are often too good to be true and can result in major losses.

- **Emotional decision-making:** Allowing feelings, such as fear or greed, to drive financial decisions can lead to bad choices. Rational and smart decision-making is important for successful investment.

- **Overconfidence:** Overestimating one's business knowledge or skills can lead to dangerous and ill-informed choices. Acknowledging the boundaries of one's knowledge and getting professional help can minimize this risk.

- **Lack of Diversification:** Focusing investments on a single product or market increases exposure to market changes. Diversifying investments across different assets and areas can reduce risk and improve stability.

Case Study of Bernard Madoff

The story of Bernard Madoff is a sharp warning of the damaging effects of poor financial choices and shady practices. Madoff's Ponzi plan not only led to his own financial ruin but also caused significant losses for thousands of investors.

Bernard Madoff was a famous investor and past head of the NASDAQ stock market. He started Bernard L. Madoff Investment Securities LLC in 1960, which became one of the biggest and most recognized firms on Wall Street. Madoff gained a reputation for giving steady and high returns to his clients, drawing a large number of private and institutional investors.

Despite his outward success, Madoff was running a Ponzi scheme, a type of investment fraud that pays returns to earlier investors using the capital of younger investors rather than from profit made by the operation of a legal business. Here's how the plan operated:

Attracting Investors: Madoff attracted investors by offering steady and high returns, which he claimed were achieved through a unique trade technique. The regular returns drew a steady stream of new buyers.

fake Reporting: To keep the image of success, Madoff gave fake account records showing successful deals and growing account amounts. In fact, no true trade was going on.

Paying Returns with New Investments: Madoff used the cash from new investors to pay returns to earlier investors. This produced the image of a good business plan and continued the scam.

Maintaining Secrecy: Madoff kept the operations of his business highly hidden and exclusive. He carefully chose clients and stopped them from taking their money, further continuing the scam.

The Ponzi plan began to unravel during the financial collapse of 2008. As market conditions worsened, buyers tried to withdraw their funds. Madoff's business could not meet the refund requests, leading to the fall of the plan. In December 2008, Madoff was caught and later admitted to the huge scam. The total costs from the plan were believed to be around $65 billion, making it one of the biggest financial frauds in history.

The Madoff case shows several important lessons for investors:

Conduct Thorough Research: Before buying, perform thorough study and due diligence. Understand the investing plan, dangers, and possible returns. Verify the validity and track record of the investing company or adviser.

Beware of Unusually High Returns: Be careful of investments that offer unusually high and steady returns with little or no risk. Such boasts are often red flags for potential scams or highly dangerous endeavors.

Verify Information: Independently verify information given by financial advisors or firms. Cross-check account records, achievement reviews, and other related papers to ensure correctness.

Diversify Investments: Diversify your financial strategy across different assets and industries. This lowers the effects of a single investment's bad performance on your total financial health.

Understand the Investment: Ensure you fully understand the investment, including how it produces profits and the related dangers. Avoid purchases that are overly complicated or unclear.

Seek Professional Advice: Consult with famous and independent financial experts. Professional advice can provide useful insights and help handle complicated financial settings.

watch assets Regularly: Regularly review and watch your assets. Stay informed about market conditions, results, and any changes in the investing plan.

To make informed and wise financial choices, consider the following practical steps:

Educate yourself: Invest time in learning about different financial choices, tactics, and risks. Financial knowledge is important for making informed choices.

Set clear investment goals: Define specific financial goals and timelines. Determine your risk tolerance and investment timeline to lead your financial strategy.

Develop a Diversified Portfolio: Build a diversified portfolio that includes a mix of assets, such as stocks, bonds, real estate, and investment funds. Diversification helps reduce risk and improve results.

Conduct due diligence: Thoroughly study possible investments and investing firms. Verify their track record, image, and legal compliance.

Avoid Emotional Decision-Making: Make business choices based on logical research rather than feelings. Avoid making hasty choices driven by fear or greed.

Monitor and Review: Regularly review your financial assets and make changes as needed. Stay updated about market trends, economic situations, and any changes in your financial position.

Chapter 7: The Environmental Influence

As I think of the tales my father shared about his friend, it's hard not to see how the surroundings played a major role in his financial breakdown. My father's friend, once a rich man, became a good example of how external factors can lead to bad financial choices.

Surrounded by peers who respected showy shows of wealth, he felt forced to match their expensive lives. This need to keep up led him to make expensive purchases, like spending $900,000 on cars for women he was never going to marry and picking up the tab for everyone at bars and restaurants. It wasn't just the big costs that added up; it was the attitude behind them.

The Power of Environmental Influences

Our surroundings can greatly affect our financial choices, often in subtle and widespread ways. From the neighborhood we live in to the friends we keep, these external factors can shape our buying habits, business choices, and general financial attitude. The urge to adapt to social norms or match the lives of those around us can lead to financial choices that are not in our best interest.

Peer Pressure and Social Comparison

One of the most powerful external effects is social pressure. We often feel the need to match the buying habits and lives of our friends, peers, and neighbors. This social comparison can lead to needless costs and poor financial choices as we try to keep up appearances.

For instance, living in a wealthy area can cause an unspoken pressure to keep a similar lifestyle. The desire to fit in and be viewed as successful can drive individuals to spend beyond their means, leading to debt and financial instability. This behavior is often referred to as "keeping up with the Joneses," where the need to match the perceived success of others overshadows sound financial reasoning.

Cultural and social standards

Cultural and social standards also play a major role in shaping our financial behavior. Certain societies place a high value on material wealth and outward shows of success, leading individuals to favor expensive purchases and extravagant lives. This societal pressure can result in financial choices driven by the desire to gain social acceptance and standing rather than long-term financial security.

In many countries, important life events such as weddings, birthdays, and holidays are marked with grandiose spending. The expectation to hold expensive parties can lead individuals to acquire substantial debt, risking their financial well-being in the process. The push to adapt to cultural norms and social standards can thus have a negative effect on one's financial health.

The Case of Allen Stanford

Allen Stanford's story is a warning tale of how external factors and the desire to keep a lavish lifestyle can lead to financial ruin. Stanford, once a wealthy banker, built his business on false activities, driven by his desire to match the opulent lives of his peers.

Allen Stanford was a famous investor and the head of Stanford Financial Group. He got a reputation for his expensive lifestyle, which included multiple homes, private jets, and extravagant parties. Stanford's financial empire looked respectable and highly successful, bringing investors from around the world.

However, the truth was starkly different. Stanford's wealth was built on a huge Ponzi plan, wherein he used new investors' money to pay returns to earlier investors. This fake business allowed him to keep the image of success and pay for his expensive lifestyle.

Stanford's financial choices were greatly affected by his desire to keep up with the luxurious lives of his friends. Surrounded by wealth and luxury, he felt forced to project an image of unparalleled success. This need to match the extravagant lives of those around him drove him to participate in false activities, eventually leading to his downfall.

The drive to keep his social standing and be viewed as a successful and important person trumped sound financial judgment. Stanford's case shows how environmental factors and social standards can drive people to make bad financial choices, with damaging results.

The fall of Stanford's business began when officials started analyzing his financial operations. In 2009, the U.S. Securities and Exchange Commission (SEC) charged him with organizing a huge Ponzi scam. The charges showed that Stanford had cheated investors of billions of dollars, leading to his final guilt and a 110-year jail term.

The impact from Stanford's false actions was broad and serious. Thousands of investors lost their life savings, and trust in financial institutions was further weakened. Stanford's desire to match the lavish lives of his friends not only led to his personal failure but also caused massive financial harm to countless others.

The case of Allen Stanford underscores the importance of being aware of external factors and their impact on financial choices. To prevent falling victim to these forces, try the following strategies:

- **Cultivate Financial Independence:** Develop a strong sense of financial freedom and fight the desire to conform to social pressures. Make financial choices based on your long-term goals and ideals rather than the need to keep up with others.

- **Set realistic financial goals:** Establish clear and realistic financial goals that fit with your values and interests. Focus on gaining financial security and steadiness rather than chasing a lifestyle driven by social comparison.

- **Practice careful spending:** Be aware of your spending habits and avoid needless costs driven by external factors. Evaluate each buy based on its value and needs rather than the desire to show others.

- **Surround yourself with good influences:** Surround yourself with individuals who share similar financial values and goals. Positive factors can encourage sound financial behavior and provide support in fighting social pressures.

- **Educate Yourself:** Invest time in financial education to make educated choices and build a better knowledge of financial concepts. Knowledge allows you to handle external effects with confidence and resilience.

- **Avoid Impulsive choices**: Take the time to consider the long-term consequences of your financial choices. Avoid making hasty choices driven by group pressure or social standards.

- **Seek Professional Advice:** Consult with reputable financial advisors to gain independent views and advice. Professional advice can help you make informed choices and fight the impact of external forces.

Chapter 8: The Adaptability Factor

Adaptability is one of the most important traits for survival and success, not just in the world of business, but in life itself. Whether it's creatures responding to their surroundings or people adjusting to social shifts, the ability to change and grow is key.

This concept holds true in the business world as well. Those who fail to react to changes in the market, technology, or customer behavior often face serious effects. This chapter discusses the dangers of failing to adapt, using the case study of Elizabeth Holmes and Theranos to show how resistance to change can lead to failure.

The Universal Importance of Adaptability

From the smallest microbes to the most complex human cultures, flexibility is a basic aspect of life and growth. In nature, animals that change to their surroundings thrive, while those that do not face loss. Similarly, people have always depended on their ability to create and react to changing situations to beat challenges and take chances.

In our daily lives, flexibility helps us to manage life's challenges, whether it's moving jobs, adjusting to new technologies, or dealing with unexpected events. This ability to turn and find new solutions is equally important in the financial world, where market conditions, technological improvements, and customer tastes are in constant change.

Adaptability in Financial Matters

In the business world, flexibility is important for keeping relevance and competition. Companies that fail to change often find themselves beaten by more agile rivals. Recognizing when change is important and being ready to adjust methods properly can mean the difference between success and failure.

Recognizing the Need for Change
One of the first steps in responding to change is understanding when it is important. This demands a keen knowledge of the market and an openness to new ideas and methods. Businesses must continuously watch industry trends, technological advances, and changes in customer tastes to spot chances and risks.

Embracing Innovation
Innovation is a key cause of flexibility. Companies that promote a mindset of innovation and welcome testing are better prepared to react to changes. Embracing innovation involves being open to new tools, business models, and strategies that can improve speed and effectiveness.

The Case of Elizabeth Holmes and Theranos

Elizabeth Holmes, the founder and CEO of Theranos, gives a sharp example of the effects of failing to change. Holmes's desire and vision for changing the healthcare industry with a new blood-testing tool intrigued the world. However, her failure to change to true medical and technology standards eventually led to the company's fall.

Elizabeth Holmes started Theranos in 2003 with the promise of changing blood tests. Her goal was to build a system that could run thorough tests using just a few drops of blood, making healthcare more available and cheap. Theranos quickly gained attention and drew major investments, with Holmes hailed as a genius entrepreneur.

Despite the original hype, Theranos' technology was fundamentally broken. The company failed to produce accurate and reliable test results, leading to major worries about its survival. Instead of solving these problems and changing the business model to more reasonable standards, Holmes decided to double down on her original vision.

Holmes's failure to adapt Theranos' business model to realistic medical and technology standards was a key mistake. Rather than recognizing the limits of the technology and moving to alternative solutions, she continued to push the company's powers, fooling investors, regulators, and the public.

The pressure to deliver on her lofty claims led Holmes to make increasingly risky choices. She rejected warnings from experts, dismissed critical feedback, and kept a façade of success even as the company's problems grew. Her unwillingness to change not only risked the company's future but also put patients' health at risk.

The fall of Theranos began when independent media and regulatory bodies started studying the company's claims. In 2015, The Wall Street Journal released an exposé showing the flaws and mistakes in Theranos' testing technology. This news prompted a number of probes, lawsuits, and governmental measures.

In 2018, Elizabeth Holmes and former Theranos head Ramesh "Sunny" Balwani were charged with criminal theft. The charges claimed that they had participated in a multi-million-dollar plot to scam investors, doctors, and patients. The failure of Theranos not only led to financial ruin for the company but also resulted in major legal and social effects for Holmes.

The case of Elizabeth Holmes and Theranos underscores the value of change in business. To prevent falling into similar mistakes, try the following strategies:

- **Embrace Realism:** While creative thought is important, it must be based in reality. Understand the limits of your technology or business plan and be ready to pivot when necessary.

- **Foster a Culture of Innovation:** Encourage innovation and experimentation within your company. Create an atmosphere where new ideas are accepted and workers feel empowered to offer unique solutions.

- **Seek comments:** Actively seek comments from experts, customers, and partners. Constructive feedback can provide useful insights and help spot areas where change is needed.

- **Monitor Industry Trends:** Stay updated about industry trends, technological advances, and changes in customer behavior. Use this knowledge to predict changes and proactively adjust your plans.

- **Be Transparent:** Transparency builds trust with investors, users, and workers. If challenges emerge, handle them freely and honestly rather than trying to hide them.

- **Invest in Research and Development:** Allocate resources to research and development to stay at the top of technological breakthroughs. Continuous innovation is key to keeping a competitive edge.

- **Develop backup Plans:** Prepare for possible problems by creating backup plans. Having a plan in place for different situations can help your company react effectively to unforeseen changes.

- **Promote Continuous Learning:** Encourage a mindset of continuous learning within your company. Provide chances for workers to gain new skills and information that can help to flexibility.

Chapter 9: The Psychological Battlefield

Money is not just a tool for deals; it is highly linked with our feelings, habits, and psychological well-being. The failure to understand and handle the psychological parts of money can lead to financial ruin. My father's friend, Tom, whom I mentioned in the opening, was also a victim of this. His excessive spending, driven by pride and the need to please, played a major role in his financial breakdown. This chapter discusses the effects of ignoring the psychological impact of money, using the case study of Richard Fuld, the former CEO of Lehman Brothers, whose bold risk-taking and denial of the financial crisis's impact led to the company's failure.

The Psychological Impact of Money

Money often evokes strong feelings such as fear, greed, pride, and worry. These feelings can drive our financial decisions, sometimes leading us to make choices that are not in our best interest. Understanding the psychological impact of money includes understanding how these feelings affect our behavior and creating methods to handle them successfully.

The Role of Emotions in Financial Decisions

Emotions play a major part in financial choices. For example, fear can lead to highly safe investments, while greed can drive risky bets. Pride might prevent us from admitting financial mistakes, and worry can cause us to avoid financial planning altogether. Recognizing these emotional causes is the first step in controlling their effect on our financial choices.

Tom, my father's friend, was the standard example of someone who ignored the psychological effect of money. His active spending habits were driven by a need to please others and keep an expensive lifestyle. He often paid for everyone's tab, bought expensive cars for women he barely knew, and went to foreign places without considering the long-term financial effects.

Tom's failure was not just due to his lack of financial knowledge but also his inability to handle the feelings connected with his wealth. His pride stopped him from admitting his financial mistakes, and his fear of losing his status among his peers led him to continue his careless spending. Tom's story serves as a strong lesson of the importance of knowing and controlling the psychological aspects of money.

The Case of Richard Fuld and Lehman Brothers

Richard Fuld's time as CEO of Lehman Brothers gives a clear example of the effects of ignoring the psychological impact of money. His bold risk-taking and rejection of the financial crisis's seriousness played a major role in the company's failure, which caused a global financial meltdown.

Lehman Brothers was once one of the most famous trading banks in the world. Under Richard Ford's direction, the company grew rapidly, taking on major risks to fuel growth and profits. Fuld's faith in his plans and his competitive nature drove Lehman Brothers to the top of the financial industry.

Despite numerous warning signs of an approaching financial crisis, Fuld and his executive team continued to pursue high-risk strategies. The subprime housing market, which Lehman Brothers strongly invested in, was showing clear signs of trouble. However, Fuld's pride and resistance kept him from recognizing the seriousness of the situation.

Fuld fell into several psychological mistakes that exacerbated Lehman Brothers' downfall:

- **Overconfidence**: Fuld's overconfidence in his skills and tactics led him to ignore warning signs and continue taking excessive risks.

- **Denial:** Fuld's denial of the financial crisis's impact on Lehman Brothers stopped him from taking necessary corrective measures.

- **Greed:** The chase of short-term income and personal gain trumped long-term security and sensible risk management.

- **Fear of Losing Face:** Fuld's fear of admitting mistakes and losing face in front of peers and clients added to his unwillingness to change direction.

As the financial disaster spread, Lehman Brothers found itself on the brink of failure. The company's exposure to risky subprime mortgage assets and its high leverage made it sensitive to market changes. Despite frantic efforts to secure a loan or merger, Lehman Brothers filed for bankruptcy on September 15, 2008. This event marked the biggest bankruptcy case in US history and caused a world financial crisis.

The failure of Lehman Brothers and Richard Fuld's part in it offer important lessons on the value of understanding the psychological effect of money. To avoid similar mistakes, consider the following strategies:

- **Self-Awareness:** Cultivate self-awareness to recognize your emotional causes and how they influence your financial choices. Regularly think about your motives and beliefs.

- **Seek various views:** Surround yourself with experts and colleagues who provide various views and helpful comments. Encourage open talks and question your ideas.

- **Prioritize Long-Term Stability:** Focus on long-term stability and sustainability rather than short-term wins. Avoid taking needless chances that could damage your financial future.

- **Admit Mistakes:** Develop the humility to admit mistakes and make necessary course changes. Acknowledge when methods are not working and be ready to change direction.

- **Risk Management:** Implement strong risk management techniques to reduce possible losses. Regularly examine your risk exposure and take effective steps to control it.

- **Continuous Learning:** Stay updated about market trends, economic situations, and best practices in financial management. Continuous learning can help you react to changed situations.

- **Emotional Regulation:** Practice emotional regulation methods such as awareness, meditation, and stress management to keep a clear and focused attitude.

Recap and Reflection

Each story illustrates how specific financial missteps can have profound consequences, not just for individuals but for entire economies. Here's a brief recap of the key case studies and their relevance to our everyday lives, along with the essential takeaways:

- **Case Study: Sean Quinn**
  Sean Quinn, once Ireland's wealthiest man, faced bankruptcy due to his lack of financial education and disastrous investments in Anglo Irish Bank. This highlights the importance of acquiring financial knowledge to make informed decisions.

Key Takeaway: Educate yourself about financial principles and seek professional advice to avoid costly mistakes.

- **Case Study: Vera Wang**
  Vera Wang's early financial difficulties stemmed from rapid business expansion without sustainable planning. Her story underscores the dangers of succumbing to

the urge for instant success without proper groundwork.

Key Takeaway: Balance immediate desires with long-term planning. Avoid impulsive decisions and focus on sustainable growth.

- **Case Study: Bjorgolfur Gudmundsson**
  Bjorgolfur Gudmundsson's accumulation of massive debt led to the collapse of Landsbanki and his personal bankruptcy. His experience shows how excessive borrowing can jeopardize financial stability.

Key Takeaway: Manage debt wisely and avoid over-leveraging. Develop a strategy to repay debt and maintain a healthy balance.

- **Case Study: Patricia Kluge**
  Patricia Kluge's extravagant lifestyle and poor financial management resulted in the foreclosure of her winery and bankruptcy. Her case illustrates how overspending and lifestyle inflation can undermine financial

security.

Key Takeaway: Exercise financial discipline and resist the temptation to inflate your lifestyle with increasing income. Focus on saving and investing.

- **Case Study: Bernard Madoff**
  Bernard Madoff's Ponzi scheme, which promised high returns but ultimately led to his downfall, demonstrates the dangers of poor investment choices and unethical behavior.

Key Takeaway: Thoroughly research investments, avoid schemes that sound too good to be true, and adhere to ethical practices.

- **Case Study: Eike Batista**
  Eike Batista's downfall resulted from poor financial planning and over-leveraging. His experience highlights the necessity of comprehensive financial planning and risk management.

Key Takeaway: Develop a solid financial plan, monitor it regularly, and adjust as needed to manage risks effectively.

- **Case Study: Allen Stanford**
  Allen Stanford's financial empire crumbled under the weight of his fraudulent activities, influenced by the lavish lifestyles of his peers. This case underscores how environmental pressures can lead to poor financial decisions.

Key Takeaway: Stay grounded and make decisions based on sound principles rather than succumbing to external pressures or trying to keep up with others.

- **Case Study: Elizabeth Holmes**
  Elizabeth Holmes's failure to adapt Theranos' business model to realistic standards led to the company's collapse. This illustrates the importance of adaptability in business and finance.

Key Takeaway: Be flexible and willing to adapt to changing circumstances. Regularly reassess and adjust your strategies to stay relevant and resilient.

- **Case Study: Richard Fuld**
  Richard Fuld's aggressive risk-taking and denial of the financial crisis's impact on Lehman Brothers led to a catastrophic failure. His story highlights the critical role of understanding and managing the psychological impact of money.

Key Takeaway: Recognize and manage the psychological factors influencing your financial decisions. Cultivate self-awareness and emotional regulation to maintain sound financial judgment.

Final Thoughts

The journey through these chapters has been a deep dive into the common financial pitfalls that can lead to ruin. By reflecting on the experiences of those who have faced financial downfall, we gain valuable insights into how to navigate our own financial lives. The key to avoiding these mistakes lies in continuous learning, disciplined spending, prudent investment, effective planning, adaptability, and psychological awareness.

As you move forward, remember that financial success is not just about making the right choices but also about understanding the deeper factors that drive those choices. Armed with these lessons, you can make informed decisions, avoid common pitfalls, and build a more secure and prosperous financial future.

Thank you for joining me on this journey through the mindset of broken people. May these insights serve as a guide to achieving lasting financial stability and success.

"Breaking Free from the Cycle of Poor Money Choices

"Breaking Free from the Cycle of Poor Money Choices

www.ingramcontent.com/pod-product-compliance
Lightning Source LLC
Chambersburg PA
CBHW071945210526
45479CB00002B/825